Living With Wellness

Gluten, Casein and Nightshade-Free Cooking

By Monica Pelletier, Holistic Nutritionist

For my Mother and Aunt Anna who have struggled with food allergies and intolerances. Their continuing battle for health was the inspiration for this cookbook.

Special thanks to my husband for being so supportive and encouraging; to my parents for helping out with the boys and lending a hand with editing; and Carissa and Alistair Nicol for their assistance with the cover design.

The following pages include brief overviews of the problems associated with gluten, casein and nightshades as they pertain to pain, inflammation and autoimmune responses. This book is not intended to educate the reader on diet changes. I recommend educating yourself further through research and consultation with a doctor or nutritionist.

Resources:

Pain/Inflammation Matters by Dr. Gloria Gilbère
www.gloriagilbere.com

The Gluten Connection, How Gluten Sensitivity May be Sabatoging Your Health -- And What You Can Do to Take Control NOW by Dr. Shari Lieberman
www.drshari.net

Listings for local pastured and grass-fed meat: www.eatwild.com

Find your nearest farmers market: http://search.ams.usda.gov/farmersmarkets/

Your Favorite Food May Be Your Worst Enemy
Food Immune Reactivity

If you're reading this, there's a good chance that you have a gluten, casein or nightshade allergy, sensitivity or intolerance. What you may not know is that these three types of foods have similar reactions in the body and many people who react to one of these foods often react to the others as well. Food Immunity Reactivity -- food intolerance, which is a delayed reaction from some foods or ingredients -- commonly occurs from eating gluten in wheat, barley, and rye; dairy products; and nightshades (tomato, potato, eggplant, tobacco and peppers.) Dr. Shari Lieberman, author of The Gluten Connection, explains food immune reactivity's complications:

- Symptoms are sometimes similar to those resulting from an allergic reaction, but the cause is not easily identified. Reactions to ingesting an offending food are delayed -- by hours or even days, and symptoms generally become apparent over time.

- Food immune reactivity does not involve the release of histamines. Consequently, antihistamines have no effect. There are no pills, shots or medications you can take to alleviate symptoms.

- An allergic reaction can evoke a violent effect (as in the case of anaphylaxis), but it incurs no long-term damage to organs. Food immune reactivity, on the other hand, is insidious, and has long-term effects on organs throughout the body can be devastating, even leading to premature death.

Reactions to these foods release antibodies that cause chronic inflammation eventually leading to celiac disease, arthritic problems, and immune disorders. If you can not tolerate gluten, casein or nightshades, the following recipes can help you eat wonderful dishes while staying healthy.

Gluten
Wheat, Spelt, Barley, Rye

Gluten-free is a hot food trend lately with products available at mainstream grocery stores, restaurants and even convenience stores. Is the trend just hype to sell higher priced designer foods or are our diet needs changing? My opinion is that the foods are changing, not our bodies. Wheat was a different grain 100 years ago. We have engineered the plants to grow faster, taller, with less water, in less space and with higher levels of gluten for better baking results. The new strains of wheat have become harder to digest and the higher levels of gluten have triggered immune reactions in the body.

So what is gluten? Gluten is the protein found in wheat, spelt, barley and rye. This protein is what helps breads rise, retain its shape and gives it a chewy texture. Studies have also shown that we tend to love gluten-laden foods because they contain a peptide that reacts with receptors in the brain that mimic the effects of opiate drugs such as morphine and heroine. Each bite makes us a little more addicted to breads, cakes and cookies.

If you have a gluten allergy, intolerance or sensitivity, you body is unable to process the gluten found in food and it causes your body to form antibodies to combat it. As your body unsuccessfully fights to break down gluten into a digestible amino acid, your intestinal lining becomes inflamed which may lead to celiac disease, irritable bowel syndrome, inflammatory bowel disease, GERD/heartburn, ulcers, chronic fatigue syndrome, asthma, and fibromyalgia.

What to avoid:
Breads, crackers, noodles, cereal, couscous, beer, cake, cookies, malt vinegar, soy sauce, many canned soups and gravy.

Items that are labeled "gluten-free" are safe. Some gluten-free flours include coconut, almond, rice, millet and buckwheat.

Always check food labels and ask what ingredients are in the foods you are served.

Casein
Cow Milk, Cheese, Yogurt, Ice cream

Many with a gluten allergy, sensitivity or intolerance find that they also can not tolerate casein, the protein found in cow milk. In a phenomenon called cross-reactivity, your autoimmune antibodies mistake other food proteins for the ones you can't tolerate. Because gluten and casein proteins are very similar, you are more likely to react negatively to cow milk products if you are unable to tolerate gluten.

Casein intolerance is not the same as lactose intolerance. Lactose is milk sugar found in all mammalian milk, including mother's milk. Babies are born with an enzyme, lactase, which allows their body to break down lactose during digestion. As we age, we begin to produce less or no lactase. When we eat milk, our body is unable to breakdown the milk sugar causing bloating, gas and diarrhea. Lactase enzyme tablets may be taken with dairy foods to avoid a lactose intolerance reaction.

The only way to avoid an immune reaction to casein is to completely avoid cow milk, including lactose-free milk, and foods made from cow milk. Reactions to casein are similar to those with gluten, causing a full immune response that can lead to chronic digestive issues, pain, inflammation, headaches and eczema.

What to avoid: cow milk, yogurt, ice cream, cheese, cream cheese, whipped cream, cream based soups, icing, butter with added cream, and salad dressings such as ranch and blue cheese.

Always check food labels and ask what ingredients are in the foods you are served.

Nightshades
Potatoes, Tomatoes, Eggplant and Peppers

Nightshades are foods that belong to the botanical group solanacae and alkaloids that can cause gastrointestinal and neurological disorders. The connection between nightshade foods and these disorders was first discovered by Dr. Norman F. Childers, former Professor of Horticulture at Rutgers University. His interest in inflammatory responses to nightshades grew as he noticed the pain he experienced after eating tomatoes as well as observing livestock kneeling in pain after eating weeds that contained solanine, an alkaloid chemical present in nightshade vegetables.

Today, Dr. Gloria Gilbère is an expert in healing those plagued by pain and inflammation. Author of Pain/Inflammation Matters, Dr. Gilbère explains that to rid the body of the alkaloid chemicals, you should adopt a diet that completely removes all nightshades.

Nightshades are everywhere and harder to identify than gluten and casein as many are hidden in ingredient lists as "spices, natural flavorings, seasonings, or starch." Avoid food items that do not list each and every spice and flavoring contained.

What to avoid:
Potatoes: red potatoes, Irish potatoes, baking potatoes, French fries, vodka made with potatoes, starches used in baked goods (many gluten-free items contain potato starch)
Tomatoes: all fresh tomatoes, spaghetti sauce, salsa, ketchup, BBQ sauce, steak sauce, and many other condiments contain tomatoes
Peppers: bell peppers, jalapenos, chili peppers, pimentos, hot sauces, paprika (dusted on just about everything at restaurants and added to most premixed seasonings)
Eggplants: all varieties

Sweet potatoes are not part of the nightshade family and are safe to eat. White and black pepper are also safe to eat as they are a berry and not from the pepper vegetable.

And remember: always check food labels and
ask what ingredients are in the foods you are served.

Recipes

I am pleased to share some of the many recipes that my family and I have come to enjoy. Try them, love them and savor every bite.

Starters, Soups and Small Bites

Lemon Summer Squash Salad
Crab Cups
Herbed Yogurt Cheese
Rosemary Crackers
Guacamole
Kale Chips
Prosciutto Wrapped Dates
Rosemary Shrimp Kabobs
Shrimp Spring Rolls
Pumpkin Coconut Bisque
Lentil Vegetable Soup
Turkey Frame Soup

Lemon Summer Squash Salad

1 clove garlic
Sea salt
¼ cup fresh lemon juice
½ cup olive oil
2 medium summer squash (yellow squash or zucchini)
Fresh ground black pepper
4 cups arugula
½ cup fresh parsley
½ cup chopped chives
¼ cup shaved hard goat cheese

Using the flat side of a knife, mash garlic into paste with a pinch of sea salt.
Place paste in a small bowl and whisk in lemon juice. Let sit for 5 minutes then whisk in olive oil to make a vinaigrette dressing.
Slice squash into thin ovals with a sharp knife or mandoline.
Put squash in a bowl and season with salt and pepper then toss with half of the vinaigrette .
Combine arugula, parsley and chives in a separate bowl and toss with remaining vinaigrette to lightly coat.
Layer arugula and squash and top with goat cheese shavings.

Arugula contains approximately the same amount of calcium as spinach but is lower in oxalates, a substance that inhibits calcium absorption. If you're looking for another great food to increase your calcium intake, arugula is a wonderful choice with 125 mg of calcium per cup.

Cucumber Crab Cups

1 hot house cucumber
¼ cup fresh crab
1 teaspoon fresh lime zest
1 teaspoon fresh lime juice
1 tablespoon green onion, sliced very thin
¼ cup celery finely chopped
1 tablespoon olive oil
sea salt
fresh cracked black pepper

Chopped chives for garnish

Cut the unpeeled cucumber into 1 ½ inch slices. With the cucumber slice laying on it's
side, make a diagonal cut creating two diagonal cucumber pieces.
Use a melon baller to remove cucumber centers to make a cup.
Lightly salt each cucumber cup and place on a towel to drain.
Mix all remaining ingredients in a bowl. Season to taste with salt and pepper.

If not serving immediately, refrigerate cups and filling separately.

To finish, place a small amount of crab filling in each cup and garnish with chives.

Invited to a party? Let the host know that you'd love to bring an appetizer or side dish. This is
not only a thoughtful gesture, but it also ensures that there is at least one dish on the table that
you can eat. But be prepared for party-goers to gobble up the food you bring, they seem to
have a radar for good food, too!

Herbed Yogurt Cheese and Rosemary Crackers

Herbed Yogurt Cheese

1 cup plain goat yogurt
1 teaspoon dried basil
½ teaspoon dried oregano
¼ teaspoon garlic powder
¼ teaspoon black pepper
¼ teaspoon sea salt

cheese cloth

Mix all ingredients.
Line a fine mesh strainer with two layers of cheese cloth.
Place yogurt mixture into the strainer on top of the cheese cloth. Fold extra cheese cloth over yogurt to cover.
Balance strainer over a bowl to allow water to drip from yogurt.
Refrigerate for 24-48 hours.
Remove cheese from strainer and cheese cloth and serve with crackers or vegetables.

Rosemary Crackers

2 cups blanched almond meal
2 tablespoons fresh finely chopped rosemary
½ teaspoon black pepper
¾ teaspoon sea salt
1 tablespoon olive oil
2 tablespoons water

Preheat oven to 350°
Combine almond meal, rosemary, black pepper and sea salt in a large bowl.
Add olive oil and water to almond meal mixture and form into a dough ball.
Place dough ball between two peices of parchment paper and roll out to ⅛ inch thickness.
Remove top parchment paper and transfer bottom paper with dough to a cookie sheet.
Cut in to 2 inch squares and bake for 10 minutes or until lightly browned.
Cool on cookie sheet for 20-30 minutes.

Guacamole

Guacamole

1 ripe avocado
1 clove minced garlic
Juice of ½ a lime
1 tablespoon fresh cilantro
sea salt to taste

Combine all ingredients and enjoy with organic corn chips or with your favorite tacos.

Kale Chips

1 bunch fresh kale
olive oil
sea salt

Preheat oven to 300°
Wash and dry kale.
Remove middle rib of each leaf and tear kale into chip sized pieces.
Drizzle olive oil over kale and toss to coat well.
Arrange kale peices on a large baking sheet so pieces are not touching.
Lightly salt kale.
Bake for 10-15 minutes. Watch closely as they can burn quickly. Chips should stay green with a slight browning of the edges.

TIP: Keep the moisture packets that come in your vitamin bottles. Add them to the air-tight container you use to store kale chips and the chips will stay crisp for a long time.

Prosciutto Wrapped Dates

1 package of dates
¼ pound of thinly sliced prosciutto
small block of manchango cheese (sheep's milk)

Preheat oven to 350°
Slice cheese into pieces about the length of the dates.
Make a lengthwise cut into dates to access and remove pits.
Place cheese inside dates.
Wrap each date with a slice of prosciutto.
Bake for 8-10 minutes or until cheese is melted.
Allow to cool briefly before serving.

Often called nature's candy, dates also deliver a good dose of healthy. Dates contain calcium, magnesium, potassium and vitamin A. Dates also contain more antioxidants than any other dried fruit while also delivering a fiber in a sweet treat.

Rosemary Shrimp Kabobs

1 pound fresh shrimp, peeled with tails on
2 cloves garlic, minced
Juice from 1 lemon
Olive oil
Sea salt
Fresh cracked pepper
6-10 sprigs fresh rosemary

Combine shrimp, garlic, lemon, olive oil, salt and pepper and allow to marinate for 30 minutes to 2 hours.
Remove leaves from rosemary, leaving an inch of leaves at the tip of each sprig.
Using the sprigs as skewers, place 3-4 shrimp on each sprig.
Grill over medium heat until shrimp are cooked through and pink.
Serve with dipping sauce.

Dipping sauce:
Juice from 1 lemon
1 clove garlic, minced
1 tablespoon olive oil
¼ teaspoon sea salt
¼ teaspoon black pepper

Whisk together all ingredients to combine.

Rosemary contains two acids, caffeic acid and rosmarinic acid, which are helpful in reducing inflammation that contributes to asthma, liver disease and heart disease. Rosemary is also mildly antiviral and antibiotic. If you live in the south, plant a rosemary bush for year-round recipies and a fragrant landscape.

Shrimp Spring Rolls

1 package dried rice noodles
1 package rice wrappers
fresh mint leaves
fresh basil leaves
8-12 peeled, cooked shrimp, sliced lengthwise
1 ½ cups finely sliced cabbage
1 cup carrots, cut into matchsticks

Dipping sauce:
juice from 1 lime
1 teaspoon fresh grated ginger
1 tablespoon fish sauce

Combine and chill.

Place the rice noodles in a large bowl of hot water until cooked, about 15 minutes.
Drain and rinse with cold water.
Make each spring roll individually before moving on to the next.
Fill a large bowl with hot water, and soak the rice wrapper sheet until slightly softened, but still rather firm; about 10-15 seconds.
Place the sheet on a large dish cloth.
Place a mint or basil leaf into the center of wrapper.
Place two shrimp halves over the mint or basil leaf, top with a small handful of the noodles, a few carrot matchsticks and cabbage.
Roll burrito style, by folding the bottom of the wrapper over the filling in the center. Fold in the left and right sides, then roll the entire package away from you tightly.
Serve with dipping sauce.

TIP: Ask where your shrimp were caught. Shrimp imported from Asia have been known to contain many toxic chemicals. Buy fresh local shrimp when possible or frozen shrimp from the United States.

Pumpkin Coconut Bisque

2 tablespoons coconut oil
1 cup chopped onion
3 cloves garlic, chopped
3 cups cooked pumpkin
2 cups chicken broth
1 teaspoon sugar
½ teaspoon allspice
1 ½ cups unsweetened coconut milk
Sea salt and pepper to taste
Shredded coconut

Melt coconut oil in a large stockpot over medium heat.
Add onion and garlic and cook until lightly browned, about 8 minutes.
Add pumpkin, broth, sugar and allspice. Bring to a boil.
Reduce heat, cover and simmer for 30 minutes.
Using a stick-blender, puree soup.
Stir in coconut milk.
Season with salt and pepper to taste.
Garnish with shredded coconut.

Pumpkin isn't just for Thanksgiving pies. This large squash is a potassium powerhouse. One cup of mashed pumpkin contains 564mg of potassium, about 33% more than one medium banana. Eating more potassium-rich foods has been linked to lower stroke risks as well as increasing bone density.

Finding pumpkin year-round may be a challenge when it's not pumkin pie season. Stock your pantry with cans when they go on sale during the fall months and you can enjoy pumpkin coconut bisque throughout the year.

Lentil Vegetable Stew

1 ¼ cups lentils, rinsed
4 cups chicken broth
1 cup water
2 cups peeled and cubed sweet potatoes
½ cup chopped celery
2 cloves minced garlic
2 teaspoons tamari soy sauce
2 teaspoons cumin
1 teaspoon coriander
Sea salt to taste
1 ½ cups zucchini or yellow squash
1 ½ cups broccoli florets

In a large pot, combine lentils and 3 cups broth and bring to a low boil.
Reduce heat to medium-low, partially cover and simmer until lentils are barely tender, 20-30 minutes.
Add remaining broth, water, sweet potatoes, onion, garlic, tamari, and spices.
Cook partially covered for 40 minutes on medium.
Add more water if soup is too thick.
Taste and adjust seasoning.
Add squash and broccoli and cook for an additional 10 minutes until vegetables are tender.

Want even more vegetables? Add frozen spinach and corn with the squash and broccoli.

Turkey Frame Soup

1 meaty turkey frame
8 cups of water
1 large onion, quartered
2 cloves garlic, minced
1 teaspoon sea salt
1 teaspoon parsley
1 teaspoon oregano
1 teaspoon marjoram
1 teaspoon black pepper
1 cup sliced carrot
1 cup sliced celery
1 cup chopped onion

optional:
1-2 cups cooked wild rice
1-2 cups cooked elbow or penne rice noodles

Place turkey frame into a large stock pot, breaking into smaller peices if neccessary to fit.
Cover with water and add quartered onion, garlic and salt.
Bring to a boil and reduce heat. Cover and simmer for 1 ½ hours.
Remove turkey frame from pot. When cool enough to handle, remove meat from bones and chop into bite-sized peices and return to pot.
Add herbs, black pepper, carrots, celery and chopped onion.
Return to boil and reduce heat. Cover and simmer for 20-25 minutes or until vegetables are cooked but still crisp.
Season to taste with salt.

Optional: add cooked wild rice or rice noodles after soup is cooked for a heartier meal.

Sensational Side Dishes

Sautéed Corn
Green Beans and Bacon
Sweet and Savory Kale
Millet Corn Bread
Sage Butternut Squash
German Red Cabbage
Sweet and Sour Bok Choy
Mexican Bean Salad
Arugula with Honey and Pine Nuts
Carrot Slaw

Sautéed Corn

2 tablespoons olive oil
1 small white onion, diced
3 ears fresh corn, kernals cut off cob
1 tablespoon fresh basil, chopped
salt
black pepper

Heat oil over medium heat in skillet.
Add onions and cook until transulcent.
Add corn to pan and cook, stirring occationally, until tender.
Stir in basil and cook for an additional minute.
Salt and pepper to taste.

Green Beans and Bacon

3 slices of bacon, cut in to small pieces
1 small onion, diced
1 pound of fresh green beans, washed and cut in to 1-2 inch pieces

Cook bacon in skillet until cooked but still soft.
Add onion and cook until translucent.
Stir in green beans and cook over medium heat until beans are cooked through but still crisp.

TIP: Always check bacon labels. If the ingredients listed include paprika, spices or natural flavoring, do not buy as these may be nightshades. There are several natural bacon brands that do not contain nightshades that are available at national grocery stores.

Sweet and Savory Kale

2 tablespoons coconut oil
1 small onion, diced
2 cloves of garlic, minced
1 tablespoon grainy Dijon mustard
4 teaspoons sugar
1 tablespoon apple cider vinegar
1 ½ cups chicken broth
4 cups stemmed, rinsed, torn kale
salt and black pepper to taste

Heat coconut oil in a large pan over medium heat.
Stir in onions and garlic, cooking until onions are translucent.
Stir in mustard, sugar, vinegar and chicken broth. Bring to a boil over high heat.
Stir in kale, cover and cook for 15 minutes, stirring occationally until tender.
Season with salt and pepper to taste.

Of all the greens, kale is the superstar. One cup of kale contains 36 calories, 5 grams of fiber, 15% of the daily requirement of calcium and vitamin B6 (pyridoxine), 40% of magnesium, 180% of vitamin A, 200% of vitamin C, and 1,020% of vitamin K. It is also a good source of minerals: copper, potassium, iron, manganese, and phosphorus.

Kale also helps lower blood cholesterol and reduce the risk of heart disease, especially when cooked instead of raw.

Millet Cornbread

1 cup blue cornmeal
½ cup millet flour
2 cups unsweetened almond milk
6 large egg yolks
4 tablespoons water
2 tablespoons olive oil
1 teaspoon sea salt
6 large egg whites, stiffly beaten

Preheat oven to 325°
Grease a 9x13 glass baking dish.
Combine cornmeal and almond milk in a saucepan and cook over medium-high, stirring constantly until the mixture thickens.
Remove from heat and cool to lukewarm.
In a separate bowl, blend egg yolks, water, oil and sea salt.
Add millet flour to yolk mixture.
Add cornmeal mash.
Gently fold in the stiffly beaten egg whites.
Pour batter into prepared dish.
Bake 40-45 minutes.

Store leftovers in refrigerator.

Corn allergies used to be extremely rare but are becoming increasingly common. Corn is added to many processed foods and are fed to the animals that become our meals. Our diets should be varied and when there is too much of one type of food, our bodies can become sensitive to that food. Rotate your diet to remain healthy!

Sage Butternut Squash

2 tablespoons olive oil
3 shallots or ½ white onion chopped
1 medium butternut squash, peeled, seeded and cut into 1/2 inch cubes
½ cup chicken broth
1 tablespoon packed brown sugar
½ teaspoon finely chopped fresh sage
1 teaspoon balsamic vinegar
Sea salt
Fresh ground black pepper

Heat oil in skillet over medium heat until hot but not smoking.
Add shallots and squash, stirring often until soft, about 5 minutes.
Add chicken broth, brown sugar, and sage. Stir until sugar is dissolved.
Cover and simmer for 8-10 minutes until squash is tender.
Remove from heat and stir in balsamic vinegar.
Season to taste with salt and pepper.

Sage contains a compound, thujone, that is an effective agent against salmonella and candida. It also contains an acid that is an antioxidant and anti-inflammatory making it extremely beneficial for fighting such conditions as rheumatoid arthritis and fibromyalgia.

German Red Cabbage

1 medium head red cabbage, cored and sliced thin
2 large granny smith apples, peeled and sliced
1 medium onion, sliced into thin rings
1 ½ cups water
1 cup apple cider vinegar
½ cup sugar
1 tablespoon coconut oil
1 teaspoon salt

6 whole peppercorns
2 whole allspice
2 whole cloves
1 bay leaf

Place cabbage, apples, onion, water, vinegar, sugar, oil and salt in a large pot or Dutch oven.
Place peppercorns, allspice, cloves and bay leaf on a double thickness of cheesecloth. Bring corners of cloth up and tie with string to form a spice bag.
Add spice bag to pot.
Bring to a boil and reduce heat. Cover and simmer for 1 ¼ hours.
Remove and discard spice bag before serving.

Sweet and Sour Bok Choy

2 tablespoons coconut oil
½ large red onion
1 head of bok choy, washed trimmed and cut into 1 inch pieces
¼ cup packed brown sugar
¼ cup red wine vinegar
½ teaspoon fresh ginger, minced
1 tablespoon cornstarch
1 tablespoon tamari soy sauce
½ cup water

Heat coconut oil in large skillet over high heat.
Add bok choy and onions and stir for 1 minute.
In a seperate bowl, combine sugar, vinegar and ginger. Add to skillet and reduce heat to medium.
Cover and steam for 1 minute.
In a seperate bowl, combine tamari, cornstarch and water. Add to skillet and stir until thickened.

Ginger has been a remedy for nausea and upset stomach for centuries. Studies are now finding this root has many other benefits which include lowering cholesterol, inhibiting the growth of colorectal cancer cells, lowering inflammation for patients with fibromyalgia and arthritis as well as acting as a antimicrobial and antivirus.

Mexican Bean Salad

1 15-ounce can black beans
1 15-ounce can kidney beans
1 15-ounce can pinto beans
1 15-ounce can great northern or cannellini beans
2 cups frozen corn
1 small red onion, finely chopped
2 cloves garlic, minced
½ cup olive oil
½ cup red wine vinegar
2 tablespoons lime juice or juice from 1 lime
1 tablespoon lemon juice or juice from ½ lemon
1 ½ tablespoons sugar
1 tablespoon sea salt
¼ cup fresh cilantro, chopped
1 ½ tablespoons ground cumin
½ tablespoon black pepper

Rinse and drain all beans.
In a large bowl, combine beans, corn, garlic and red onion.
In a separate bowl, whisk together olive oil, vinegar, lemon and lime juices, sugar, salt,
cilantro, cumin and black pepper.
Pour olive oil dressing over bean mixture and gently stir to combine.
Refrigerate and serve cold.
Best if made a day in advance to allow beans to absorb dressing.

Arugula with Honey and Pine Nuts

1 teaspoon olive oil
2 tablespoons pine nuts
1 pound arugula
¼ teaspoon sea salt
2 tablespoons honey

Heat oil in a pan over medium heat.
Add pine nuts, cooking and stirring frequently until nuts begin to brown.
Add arugula, cooking and stirring frequently.
As the arugula begins to wilt, stir in honey and salt.

Carrot Slaw

¾ pound carrots, peeled and shaved with a vegetable peeler
4 scallions, thinly sliced
1 tablespoon olive oil
2 tablespoons rice vinegar
1 tablespoon sesame seeds
Zest from 1 lime
1 tablespoon fresh lime juice
Sea salt
Black pepper

Combine carrots, scallions, oil, vinegar, sesame seeds, lime zest and juice.
Season with salt and black pepper.
Toss to combine.
Serve at room temperature or chilled.

Main Dishes

Bacon Zucchini Frittata
Maple Roasted Chicken with Sweet Potatoes
Mahi with Mango Salsa
A Very Nice Pot Roast
Green Coconut Chicken
Fish Cakes
Southern Comfort Pork Chops
Ginger Shrimp and Quinoa
Orange Glazed Chicken Stirfry
Lemon Rosemary Stuffed Chicken

Bacon Zucchini Frittata

10 eggs
1 ½ cups cheddar goat cheese, shredded
¼ teaspoon black pepper
4 slices bacon, cut into small pieces
1 small onion, diced
1 clove garlic
1 small zucchini, finely diced

In a large mixing bowl, gently beat eggs. Add cheese and black pepper, set aside.
In a large skillet, cook bacon until slightly crispy, pour off fat.
Add onion to skillet with bacon and cook until translucent.
Add garlic and zucchini to skillet and cook just until zucchini starts to soften.
Pour egg mixture into skillet and cook over medium heat.
As egg mixture begins to set, gently stir so uncooked eggs flow underneath.
Continue cooking until egg mixture is almost set, surface will still be moist.
Place skillet under broiler for 2-3 minutes until top is just set.

Eggs contain choline, an essential nutrient for cardiovascular and brain function. Found in the egg yolk, choline helps prevent the accumulation of cholesterol and fat in the liver. Choline also helps lower homocysteine, a risk factor for heart disease. This nutrient is also needed in the synthesis of one of the major neurotransmitters in the body, acetylcholine, which is critical for memory and thought.

Maple Roasted Chicken with Sweet Potatoes

4-8 bone-in chicken thighs
1 large white onion cut into wedges
4 large sweet potatoes, peeled and cut into cubes
2 tablespoons olive oil
1 teaspoon sea salt
¼ teaspoon black pepper
3 tablespoons maple syrup
6 sprigs fresh thyme or 1 tablespoon dried thyme

Preheat oven to 400°
Rinse chicken and pat dry.
Arrange chicken, onions and sweet potatoes in large baking dish.
Drizzle with olive oil.
Season with salt and pepper. Toss to coat.
Drizzle with maple syrup and top with thyme.
Roast in oven, stirring once, until chicken is cooked through-about 1 hour.

Sweet potatoes are part of the morning glory family and are not actually potatoes. This starchy vegetable is full of soluble fiber and packed with antioxidants including beta-carotene. Loaded with vitamin A, sweet potatoes also contain calcium, potassium and a powerful anti-inflammatory, quercetin.

Mahi with Mango Salsa

Mahi

1 pound of mahi cut in to 2-4 steaks
1 teaspoon cumin
¼ teaspoon garlic powder
½ teaspoon sea salt
½ teaspoon black pepper
olive oil

Combine cumin, garlic powder, sea salt and black pepper.
Drizzle mahi with olive oil and dust with cumin mixture.
Grill over medium high heat until fish is flakey.
Top with mango salsa.

Mango Salsa

1 fresh mango cut into ½ inch cubes
1 cup fresh pineapple cut in to ½ inch cubes
½ small red onion diced
2 garlic cloves minced
2 tablespoons fresh cilantro roughly chopped
sea salt
black pepper

Combine all ingredients and season with salt and black pepper to taste.
Best if prepared 1-2 hours before serving to allow flavors to combine.

A Very Nice Pot Roast

2-3 pound pot roast
Grapeseed oil
4 sprigs fresh thyme
4 sprigs fresh rosemary
2 bay leaves
1 white onion sliced into half inch rounds
1 bottle malbec red wine
1 pint beef stock
Sea salt
Fresh cracked black pepper

Preheat oven to 350°
Heat grapeseed oil in dutch oven over high heat.
Very generously salt and pepper each side of roast.
Sear each side of roast in dutch oven until meat is very custy, about 6-7 minutes per side.
Remove roast from dutch oven and set aside.
Reduce heat to medium low and sweat onions and herbs until translucent but not brown.
Deglaze pan with half the bottle of wine (save the rest for dinner!)
Add roast back to dutch oven and add enough beef stock to cover meat halfway.
Cover and place in oven for 2 ½ hours.
Carefully flip roast half-way through cooking.

Best when allowed to cool, refrigerated and reheated the next day.

Sautéed Corn (pictured) recipe on page 32

Green Coconut Chicken

3 tablespoons grapeseed or coconut oil
½ cup sliced fresh ginger
4-6 chicken pieces bone-in
sea salt
freshly ground black pepper
2 14-ounce cans coconut milk
1 10-ounce package frozen chopped spinach, thawed and drained
1 thinly sliced yellow summer squash

Cooked brown rice

Heat oil in a large skillet over medium heat.
Stir in ginger slices, cooking until fragrant and lightly browned. Remove ginger and set aside.
Season chicken with salt and pepper.
Place chicken in the same skillet over medium-high heat. Cook until chicken is lightly browned on all sides.
Return ginger to skillet and add coconut milk. Bring to a boil and cover with the lid tilted to allow steam to escape.
Reduce heat to medium-low and simmer until chicken is no longer pink at the bone, about 30 minutes.
Add spinach and squash. Simmer uncovered until vegetables are warmed through, 8-12 minutes.
Season with salt and pepper to taste.
Serve over brown rice.

Fish Cakes

3-4 tablespoons peanut oil
2-3 filets of cooked fish (or 1 can, drained)
1 small onion, diced
½ cup gluten-free bread crumbs
1 egg
1 teaspoon parsley
1 teaspoon garlic powder
½ teaspoon black pepper
½ teaspoon sea salt

Heat oil in a large skillet over medium-high heat.
Gently mix all other ingredients, keeping chunks of fish intact.
Scooping large spoonfuls of the mixture, use your hands to make patties.
Place patties in oil and cook until first side is browned, turn patties browning second side.
Remove patties from pan and place on a paper towel lined plate to remove some oil.
Serve hot.

Many people don't like eating fish that is left over from the day before. Fish Cakes are a great way to enjoy the fish instead of letting it go to waste. They're wonderful on top of a salad with a vinaigrette dressing.

Southern Comfort Pork Chops

4 center cut, bone-in, rib pork chops
2 teaspoons sea salt
freshly ground black pepper
2 tablespoons grapeseed oil
2 tablespoons unsalted ghee (clarified butter)
¼ cup Southern Comfort or bourbon
½ cup chicken broth
1 tablespoon grainy mustard
3 tablespoons goat yogurt

Pat pork chops dry, season on one side with salt and pepper.
Preheat skillet over medium-high for about 1 minute.
Add oil and heat to shimmering.
Add pork chops to skillet, seasoned side down, and cook until browned, 4-5 minutes.
Add ghee to skillet and cook an additional minute.
Season top side of pork chops with salt and pepper then turn chops over. Continue cooking until firm, 5-6 minutes. Transfer pork chops to plate and tent with foil.
Pour fat out of skillet. Pull skillet from heat and carefully add Southern Comfort. Carefully light the alcohol with flame from stove or lighter. Return pan to heat and cook until reduced by half then add chicken broth and bring to a simmer.
Simmer for 3 minutes.
Wisk in mustard and yogurt and simmer until sauce coats the back of a spoon, 1-2 minutes.
Season to taste with salt and pepper.
Serve sauce over pork chops.

TIP: You may find the pork chops create a lot of smoke while cooking. If you don't have a well-functioning exhaust fan, cook this dish on the burner on your outdoor grill.

Ginger Shrimp and Quinoa

Shrimp:
12 to 16 cooked medium shrimp, peeled
2 tablespoons sesame oil
1 tablespoon lime juice
2 cloves garlic, minced
¼ teaspoon sea salt
¼ teaspoon white pepper

In a small bowl, combine all ingredients listed above and marinate for 30 minutes.

For the dressing:
2 tablespoons freshly squeezed lime juice
1 tablespoon rice wine vinegar
1 teaspoon minced fresh ginger
1 garlic clove, minced
2 teaspoons sesame oil
2 tablespoons melted coconut oil
¼ teaspoon white pepper
Sea salt to taste

In a small bowl, whisk together all dressing ingredients.

For the salad:
3 cups cooked quinoa
4 scallions, white and green parts, sliced thin
1 small cucumber, halved, seeded and thinly sliced on the diagonal
¼ cup chopped cilantro

In a large bowl, combine salad ingredients and shrimp. Toss with the dressing and serve.

Orange Glazed Chicken Stirfry

¾ pound chicken breast or thighs, cut in to bite-sized peices
2 tablespoons honey
2 tablespoons rice wine vinegar
Zest from 1 orange
Juice from ½ orange
1 tablespoon tamari soy sauce
1 teaspoon cornstarch
2 tablespoons coconut or grapeseed oil
1 package frozen stir-fry vegetables (check ingredients for nightshade vegetables)

Cooked rice

For sauce, mix together honey, vinegar, orange zest and juice, tamari soy sauce and cornstarch. Set aside.
Heat cooking oil in a large skillet or wik over medium-high heat.
Stir-fry vegetables in oil for 3 minutes or until tender, yet crisp. Remove vegetables from pan.
Add chicken to hot pan and stir-fry until chicken is cooked through, 3-5 minutes.
Push chicken to the sides of the pan, stir sauce and add to the center of the pan. Cook and stir sauce until thick and bubbly.
Return vegetables to pan. Stir vegetables, chicken and sauce until all is coated and heated through, about 1 minute.
Serve over rice.

TIP: Cut chicken while it is still partially frozen. The harder meat is easier to handle when it is firm from the freezer.

Lemon Rosemary Stuffed Chicken

1 whole chicken
Stuffing recipe (see below)
Sea salt
Fresh ground pepper
5 sprigs fresh rosemary
2 cloves garlic, peeled
1 lemon

For stuffing, combine:
1 cup dried gluten-free bread crumbs
1 ¾ cups coconut oil
2 tablespoons freshly grated lemon zest
sea salt
freshly ground pepper

Preheat oven to 400°
Starting from the neck end of the chicken, carefully run your finger under the skin to seperate from the meat, leaving it attatched in the center to the sternum. Do not tear the skin.
Evenly work stuffing under the skin of the legs and breast.
Season inside of chicken with salt and pepper. Place rosemary and garlic inside the cavity of the chicken.
Prick lemon all over with the tines of a fork and add to the cavity.
Roast chicken until juices run clear, about 1 hour.
Remove from oven and cover with foil. Allow to rest for 20 minutes before carving.

Sweet Treats:
Breakfast, Snacks and Desserts

Orange Cranberry Muffins
Banana Bread
Chocolate Oat Bites
Coconut Macaroons
Chocolate Cinnamon Caramel Corn
Purple Velvet Chocolate Bites
Almond Pumpkin Bars
Lemon Meringue Pie
Peach Crisp
Chocolate Coconut Ice Cream
Coffee Coconut Ice Cream

Orange Cranberry Muffins

1 ¼ cups rice flour
¼ cup tapioca flour
⅔ cup brown sugar
2 teaspoons baking powder
1 teaspoon baking soda
¼ teaspoon fine sea salt
⅔ cup plain goat yogurt
⅔ cup orange juice
zest from 1 orange
1 ¼ cups frozen cranberries

Optional: demerara or brown sugar for sprinkling

Preheat oven to 400°
Combine flour, sugar, baking powder, baking soda and salt.
In a seperate bowl, combine yogurt, orange juice and zest.
Sprinkle cranberries with flour mixture and toss to coat to prevent berries from sinking during baking.
Combine wet and dry mixtures and fold in cranberries.
Fill greased or lined muffin tins ⅔ full.
Optional: sprinkles tops with demerara or brown sugar.
Bake 20-25 minutes or until a toothpick inserted in middle muffin comes out clean.
Makes 12 muffines.

TIP: Buy cranberries when they are in season and on sale around Thanksgiving. Throw the whole bag in the freezer. Cranberries freeze well and you'll save money buying in-season.

Banana Bread

1 ¼ cups rice flour
¼ cup tapioca flour
1 ½ teaspoons baking powder
¼ teaspoon baking soda
½ teaspoon ground cinnamon
Pinch of salt
1 egg
3 medium bananas, mashed
¾ cup sugar
¼ cup coconut oil or other cooking oil
1 teaspoon vanilla extract
1 teaspoon finely shredded lemon peel
½ cup toasted chopped pecans or walnuts

Preheat oven to 350°
Grease an 8x4x2 loaf pan and set aside.
In a medium mixing bowl, combine rice flour, baking powder, baking soda, cinnamon and salt, set aside.
In a seperate bowl, combine egg, bananas, sugar, oil, vanilla and lemon peel.
Add egg mixture to dry mixture all at once. Stir until just moistened (batter will still be lumpy). Fold in nuts.
Pour batter into prepared pan.
Bake for 50-55 minutes or until a toothpick inserted near center comes out clean.
Cool for 10 minutes before removing from pan.

Toast and drizzle with honey before serving.

TIP: Use very ripe bananas for the best flavor. Banana bread is a great go-to when you have leftover bananas that are riper than you'd like to eat on their own.

Peanut Butter Oat Bombs

2 cups gluten free oats
1 cup peanut butter (smooth or crunchy)
1 ½ cups coconut flakes
1 cup freshly ground flax seed
1 cup dark chocolate chips
½ cup honey
2 teaspoons vanilla extract

Optional: ½ cup chia seeds, dried fruits or toasted nuts

Combine all ingredients in a stand mixer with paddle attachment on low speed.
Cover and refrigerate for 30 minutes.
After thoroughly chilled, form into bite-sized balls.
Refrigerate in an airtight container or freeze.
If freezing, allow to thaw in refrigerator before eating.

Can't eat peanuts? There are several other nut and seed butters that can be substituted for peanut butter. Look for those made with almonds, cashews or sunflower seeds.

Coconut Macaroons

1 teaspoon almond extract
1 14 ounce package sweetened shredded coconut
4 large egg whites
Pinch of salt
Dash of cream of tartar
½ cup sugar

Optional: dark chocolate, nuts

Preheat oven to 350°
Combine almond extract and coconut in a bowl.
In a seperate bowl, beat egg whites and salt until they begin to stiffen.
Add sugar to egg whites in 3 parts and continue to whip until whites are very stiff.
Fold coconut mixture in to egg whites.
On a parchment lined cookie sheet, drop teaspoons of the mixture, leaving 1-2 inches between each macaroon.
Cook for 15 or until the macaroons begin to brown on top.

Optional:
Before cooking, add nuts to the top of the macaroons.
After cooling, dip the bottoms of macaroons in dark chocolate (check packaging to ensure no milk products are present,)

Chocolate Cinnamon Caramel Corn

12 cups popped popcorn (about ½ cup kernels)
1 cup pecans toasted and chopped
1 cup brown sugar
¾ teaspoon cinnamon
¼ cup honey
½ cup coconut oil
1 teaspoon vanilla
½ teaspoon baking soda

½ cup dark chocolate chips

Preheat oven to 250°
Place popcorn and pecans in a very large bowl and set aside.
Combine brown sugar and cinnamon in a glass bowl. Mix well.
Place coconut oil on top of sugar mixture, pour honey on top of oil.
Microwave on high for 30 seconds then stir to combine. Return to microwave and heat for 2 minutes. Remove, stir and return to microwave and heat for an additional 2 minutes.
Remove from microwave, add vanilla and baking soda. Stir to combine. Mixture will foam and rise.
Pour caramel mixture over popcorn and pecans and stir well to coat.
Spread popcorn mixture onto parchment paper-lined cookie sheet. Bake for 30 minutes, stirring every 10 minutes.
Remove from oven and spread out on to a large piece of parchment.
Melt chocolate in microwave. Drizzle over popcorn mixture.
When chocolate is hardened and popcorn is cool, break into chunks.
Store in air-tight container.

Purple Velvet Chocolate Bites

2 ½ cups grated beets
1 cup honey or maple syrup
4 eggs
½ cup coconut oil
1 tablespoon vanilla extract
½ teaspoon almond extract
½ cup cocoa powder
½ teaspoon sea salt

Preheat oven to 350°
In a small pot, bring beets and honey or maple syrup to a boil. Cover and reduce heat. Simmer for 30 minutes until beets are soft.
Puree beet mixture with stick blender until smooth.
Blend in eggs, oil, vanilla, almond extract, cocoa and salt.
Pour batter into lined cupcake pans.
Bake for 30-35 minutes until a toothpick comes out clean.
Cool and serve. Bites will stick to cupcake liners if not cool.

Bites freeze wonderfully. Remove from freezer 5-10 minutes before enjoying.

TIP: Wear rubber gloves and an apron when grating and handling beets. Beet juice can and will stain hands and clothing.

Almond Pumpkin Bars

½ cup pumpkin puree
½ cup maple syrup
2 eggs
1 cup blanched almond flour
¼ teaspoon sea salt
½ teaspoon baking soda
¼ teaspoon cinnamon
¼ teaspoon nutmeg
¼ cloves

Preheat oven to 350°
In a stand mixer, combine pumpkin, maple syrup and eggs and blend on medium for 2 minutes.
In a seperate bowl, combine almond flour, sea salt, baking soda, cinnamon, nutmeg and cloves.
Slowly add dry ingredients to the pumpkin mixture and mix for a full minute until well combined.
Pour batter into a greased 8x8 baking dish.
Bake for 30-35 minutes.

Rich in calcium, fiber, phosphorus, magnesium and vitamin E, almond flour is a nutritious substitute for wheat flour in many baking recipes. With virtually no carbohydrates, almond meal is also wonderful for those with diabetes or blood sugar issues.

Lemon Meringue Pie

Crust

2 cups blanched almond flour
2 tablespoons coconut oil

½ teaspoon celtic sea salt
1 egg

Preheat oven to 375°
Place flour and salt in food processor and pulse briefly or mix with clean hands.
Add coconut oil and egg and pulse or mix by hand until mixture forms a ball.
Press dough into a 9-inch metal tart pan.
Bake for 10 minutes, remove and set aside for filling.

Filling

4 egg yolks (reserve whites for meringue)
½ cup cornstarch
1 ⅓ cups sugar
3 tablespoons coconut oil
1 ½ tablespoons finely grated lemon zest

1 ½ cups water
¼ teaspoon salt
½ cup lemon juice

Whisk egg yolks and set aside.
In a medium saucepan, combine cornstarch, water, sugar and salt. Whisk to combine.
Over medium heat, stir frequently until mixture boils. Continue to boil for 1 minute and then remove from heat.
Gradually, one whisk-full at a time, add hot mixture to egg yolks and stir until you have added all of the hot mixture to the egg yolks.
Return egg mixture to saucepan over low heat. Cook for one minute, stirring constantly.
Remove from heat; gently stir in coconut oil, lemon juice and lemon zest until well combined.
Pour mixture into pie crust while filling is still hot. Top with meringue (below) making sure meringue covers all of filling.
Bake for 10-12 minutes or until meringue is golden. Cool completely before slicing.

Meringue Topping

4 egg whites
2 tablespoons sugar

1 pinch cream of tartar

Beat egg whites and cream of tartar until soft peaks form.
Gradually add sugar and continue beating until stiff peaks form, 1-2 minutes.
Use to top lemon filling.

Peach Crisp

5 cups of fresh peaches, peeled and sliced
2 tablespoons sugar
¾ cup gluten-free oats
½ cup packed brown sugar
Pinch of salt
¼ cup rice flour
¼ teaspoon ground cinnamon
¼ teaspoon ground ginger
Dash of nutmeg
¼ cup coconut oil

Preheat oven to 375°
Place peaches in a 2-quart square baking dish, stir in 2 tablespoons of sugar.
For topping, in a medium mixing bowl, combine oats, brown sugar. salt, rice flour, and spices.
Mix in coconut oil with a fork until topping resembles course crumbles.
Sprinkle topping over peaches.
Bake for 30-35 minutes or until fruit is tender and topping is golden.

Buy organic! Peaches are on the dirty dozen list of produce that contains the highest levels of pesticide residue. Buy organic to reduce your exposure.

The Dirty Dozen:

Apples	Grapes	Celery
Spinach	Sweet Bell Peppers	Lettuce
Peaches	Cucumbers	Strawberries
Domestic Blueberries	Imported Nectarines	Potatoes

Chocolate Coconut Ice Cream

3 cups unsweetened coconut milk (about 2 cans)
⅔ cup cocoa powder
6 tablespoons agave or maple syrup
1 teaspoon vanilla extract
pinch of salt

Whisk cocoa powder in a small amount of coconut milk, until smooth.
Mix all ingredients and whisk until well combined or combine in a blender.
Make according to your ice cream machine's instructions.
Add your favorite mix-ins and freeze.

Mix-in suggestions:
Chocolate chips + shaved coconut
Frozen banana pieces + chocolate shavings
Mini marshmallows + toasted pecans
Frozen cherries

Coffee Coconut Ice Cream

3 cups unsweetened coconut milk (about 2 cans)
2 teaspoons instant coffee
7 tablespoons agave or maple syrup
1 teaspoon vanilla extract
pinch of salt

Whisk together all ingredients until well combined or combine in a blender.
Make according to your ice cream machine's instructions.

Coconut ice cream freezes very hard. Remove from freezer 10-15 minutes before serving for easier scooping.